# Glimpses of Holiness

# Glimpses of Holiness

ERMAL KIRBY
*Foreword by William J. Abraham*

RESOURCE *Publications* · Eugene, Oregon

GLIMPSES OF HOLINESS

Copyright © 2021 Ermal Kirby. All rights reserved. Except for brief quotations in critical publications or reviews, no part of this book may be reproduced in any manner without prior written permission from the publisher. Write: Permissions, Wipf and Stock Publishers, 199 W. 8th Ave., Suite 3, Eugene, OR 97401.

Resource Publications
An Imprint of Wipf and Stock Publishers
199 W. 8th Ave., Suite 3
Eugene, OR 97401

www.wipfandstock.com

PAPERBACK ISBN: 978-1-6667-1312-1
HARDCOVER ISBN: 978-1-6667-1313-8
EBOOK ISBN: 978-1-6667-1314-5

Bible quotations are taken from the *New Revised Standard Version Bible*. Copyright © 1989, Division of Christian Education of the National Council of the Churches of Christ in the United States of America;

*Good News Bible* © 1976, American Bible Society, New York

*The Amplified New Testament*, Marshall Morgan and Scott © The Lockman Foundation, 1958

07/16/21

# Contents

| | | |
|---|---|---|
| *Foreword by William J. Abraham* | | vii |
| *How to use this book* | | ix |
| *Prologue* | | xi |
| Chapter 1 | Holiness and Grace | 1 |
| Chapter 2 | Christ and Holiness | 8 |
| Chapter 3 | Holiness and Rules | 17 |
| Chapter 4 | At Peace in Holiness | 23 |
| Chapter 5 | Holiness: Debits and Credits | 29 |
| Chapter 6 | Holiness: Together on the Journey. | 36 |

# Foreword

## WILLIAM J. ABRAHAM

It has long been easy to write off Methodism ancient and contemporary as essentially over and done with. Yet one deeply informed commentator, Ferdinand Mount, wrote recently that Methodism at the grass roots devised "almost a new civilization and a refreshing of life."[1] Mount is a superb writer full of insight on a host of topics. I think he is exactly right. Hence it is crucial to keep alive the crown jewels of Methodism with its awkward but inspiring vision of holiness of heart and life. This is a tall order. Ermal Kirby has risen to the challenge in this splendid volume.

Truth be told, Ermal and his family lived next door when we were both students at Oxford. He was a model of intelligence, good humor, and realism; he also quietly exhibited the vision of holiness he seeks to articulate here. We lost touch over time, but we reconnected recently by email and I instantly sensed that he had fulfilled the promise that was so visible in his student days. So, it is a pleasure to welcome this work.

The register is important. He lodges his vision of holiness in a fine study of Colossians. This means that it is rooted in scripture; equally important it makes his work accessible to other Christians in an engaging manner. His writing is a model of short, sharp declarative sentences that grab our attention. It also takes us imaginatively

---

1. Ferdinand Mount, *English Voices, Lives, Landscapes, and Laments* (New York: Simon and Schuster, 2016), 164.

back into the world of the early Christians before relocating us firmly in our everyday lives. Hence the vision of holiness is not something abstract and out of reach but draws us naturally into its beauty and its possibilities.

Global Methodism is at a crossroads. It faces the same challenges that are rippling across the Christian world of the West. However, this is just the standard jeremiad that we should resist. Across the world Methodism and its joyful offspring, as Mount also notes, "has turned out to be the most vibrant current in religion today." Deeper still, it keeps alive the deep reasons why millions of folk become and remain Christians, for it is built on the ineradicable warrant of religious experience and the real possibility of conspicuous sanctity. It has its own intellectual treasures (and vices), but these have been overshadowed by its native optimism of grace. Perhaps this is as it should be, for Methodism at its best is a blend of primal religion and Primitive Christianity. The intellectual treasures lie below the surface and it requires hard work to excavate them.

So, I return to the primary reason to welcome this volume. It takes us to the core of our tradition. Let loose again in the format of scriptural meditations in the hearts and minds of local congregations, it is bound to bear fruit and keep alive a vital element of the Gospel.

# How to use this book

When I was minister of the Central Methodist Church in Birmingham, UK, I used to meet each week with a group of church members to look at one or more of the Lectionary readings for the next Sunday. The group was never large, but I found it one of the most fruitful experiences of my ministry as, in the fellowship that developed, members of the group shared insights from their own experiences and asked the questions that they had never before ventured to ask.

I told them that for me it was like going to the open market in the Bullring nearby and gathering items from different stalls that I would then turn into a dish that would be served to the whole church on Sunday. I'm sure that members of the group listened with particular attention to see if their particular ingredients could be detected and how they had been combined with the offering from other members.

This awareness of the treasures held by all members stayed with me and I tried in the later stages of my ministry to find ways of getting out in the open the things that were often kept hidden in the "pockets and handbags" of the minds of church members, as I believed that the whole church would be enriched by that portion of the abundant glory of Christ that each member had received or glimpsed. Open conversation is key; ensuring that no one feels that their question or concern is too trivial or too "way out" to be voiced, and often it is the quietest member of the group who will offer an insight that opens up new and creative possibilities for the whole group.

## How to use this book

So, the questions posed at the beginning of each study in this book are not the starter before the main course, they are the gathering and preparing of the raw ingredients, appreciating their uniqueness and potential and seeing how they can be used to nourish all. I suggest, therefore, that you go through these questions on your own, answering each one as fully as you can. You could find it helpful to have a notebook for your answers as in the printed book there might not be enough space beneath each question. After answering the questions for yourself, read the 'Drawing Together' section and see how the things written there relate to the answers you came up with. Add supplementary notes as appropriate—perhaps in a different colour or script.

If you are meeting as part of a group, it could be helpful if members first share their initial insights, before the group considers the material in 'Drawing Together' and sees how it supplements or challenges the ideas of the group. Some of the responses could be quite personal and it is important that every member of the group knows that they can disclose as much or as little as they choose, without any pressure from anyone else. The group could be helped if there was a note taken of key insights that could have implications for the life of the wider church. The concluding prayer of each study is offered as a way of summing up the study and making a commitment that embodies the learning.

The challenges faced by the early Christians in Colossae are ones that Christians still wrestle with today: do we rely too much on our own effort rather than on the grace of God? Do we grasp the significance of Christ for all people and for all time? What is the place of rules and regulations in the life of holiness? How does walking the way of holiness affect our relationships in our homes and at work? How can we help and support our fellow travellers as we journey together into the fulness of life that is God's will for all people?

I trust that as you explore these questions you too will catch glimpses of holiness and that you will be drawn closer to the Holy God who calls us all.

# Prologue

It was Sunday evening, and in Colossae the followers of Jesus were making their way to the home of Philemon[1]. They had been meeting there for some time–partly because it was a good location that people from all around the city could get to quite easily; partly, because it was one of the bigger houses and had a patio that opened onto lovely gardens, which meant that quite a large number of people could get together–some would be standing or sitting in the dining area, some on the outside stairs leading up to the rooms on the flat roofs, and some out on the patio; and they also liked meeting at Philemon's house because he and his wife offered such wonderful hospitality you always felt very much at home; well actually, even better than being at home!

Tonight, there was a special buzz of excitement as the Christ-ones gathered. News had spread that Tychicus had returned from Rome and that he had brought (would you believe it?) a letter from the Apostle Paul addressed to them personally–to them, in little old Colossae, and with the Apostle's autograph at the end. They could hardly believe it. So, they came: the best turn-out there had been for ages; definitely a case of standing room only.

It was a very mixed gathering: people were there who had followed the Jewish religion (and some who still did, trying to combine it with their belief in Jesus as the Messiah); and some who had lived lives without giving a thought to any kind of religious obligation–eat, drink and be merry, for tomorrow you die; some who

---

1. I have used 'Philemon' for convenience, as he is widely regarded as a leader within the churches in the Lycus Valley—Laodicea, Hierapolis and Colossae.

were important figures in the city–traders, landowners, members of the academy; and some who were farm labourers and house slaves.

They all came; some in good time, because they could plan their day; some very late, because Sunday was a normal working day and they had to finish their work before they could get away–and you know you can never find a donkey-taxi to hitch a ride when you most need one!

One of the first to arrive was 'father' Maccabaeus. He had been part of the gathering in Colossae from its very beginning. He loved to tell how, as a young man, he had made that once-in-a-lifetime journey to Jerusalem for the Passover and had stayed on for three months, lodging with his mother's relatives who lived in the city. He had been there on the day of Pentecost, crowded into the temple courts and had heard the message of the group of rough looking Galileans who claimed that the Messiah had come and was none other than Jesus of Nazareth who had been executed as a common criminal barely seven weeks earlier. He had found his heart strangely warmed by the message, and before he knew it, he was pressing forward to be one of the first to be baptised as a follower of the Way. He described it as the day when he found fulfilment.

A whole group of younger people were the next to arrive at Philemon's house: full of life, full of questions, the gathering was their weekly opportunity to catch up with one another and to compare notes on everything, from the joys and sorrows of their domestic lives to the changes in the civic governance of Colossae. Among them were Dolores and Dimitri, newly married, very much in love, but struggling sometimes to understand one another–all very normal, really.

Caleb was the unofficial 'leader' of this group. Not that there was much leading needed; somehow, they seemed to manage to get together during the week as well as on Sundays–more often than not, for some celebration or another. Everyone liked Caleb; he was thoughtful, without being too heavy, and he would often throw into a discussion some new insight or principle that helped others to get a handle on the subject under consideration.

Dymphna arrived in a blaze of colour, bursting with energy as always. It was hard to define Dymphna; she didn't fit neatly into any category, but it was hard not to like her. Some people wondered how she held together all the different ideas that spilled out of her all the time. She had brought someone new with her (the gathering had become accustomed to the comings and goings of different people in Dymphna's life and accepted them all with good grace).

The slaves were there too. They came in two's and three's, a little hesitant, as if they couldn't quite believe that they were allowed to be there, and often not saying much, but week after week, they came. Some of them were owned by people who were also present in the gathering and neither the slaves nor the owners could quite work out how their relationship with Christ should affect their relationships with one another.

And, of course, the children were there, running around, having fun, not sure what it all meant, but knowing for sure that they too belonged to the Christ-ones, because they had been baptized. There was even a rumour that the Apostle had included a special message for them.

Philemon and Apphia[2] welcomed everyone, and Euphonos led the singing of a new hymn that he had just written in praise of the Jesus, the Master. (The words were fine, but not everyone could follow the tune and some thought that it would have gone better with a flute rather than one of those multi-stringed new-fangled instruments.)

There followed a time when anyone could say a bit about how they were getting on as they tried to live as followers of Jesus each day, and to ask for the help of their fellow believers. That was mixed with the singing of Psalms and other songs that they knew.

Then Philemon stood up again. "Brothers and Sisters," he said, "I'm sure that you all know by now that we have received a letter from our beloved and faithful brother, the missionary and Apostle, Paul. Some years ago, our brother was involved in outreach work that centred on Ephesus about a hundred and thirty kilometres from here; and it was that mission activity that inspired our own dear brother Epaphras to start an assembly here in Colossae. The

---

2. See the letter to Philemon, verse 2.

Apostle never made it to our City, but tonight we have the next best thing, a letter from him.

"I have asked our brother, Merring-Petros, from the local Academy to read the letter for us. As you know, he is a man of letters himself and he has a good strong voice which means you will all be able to hear."

Philemon sat down and Merring-Petros stood up and began to read: "Paul, an apostle of Christ Jesus by the will of God, and Timothy our brother, to the Saints and faithful brothers and sisters in Christ–in Colossae: Grace to you and peace from God our Father."

Merring-Petros paused, partly for dramatic effect (he was like that) and partly because there was, first, an audible gasp, and then some whispers and murmurs from the assembly. "Did you hear that?" someone asked, "The Apostle called us 'the holy ones, saints, God's own people'; us, you and me, here in Colossae! Wasn't that how the Jews described themselves, as God's chosen ones? Ask old father Maccabaeus over there. And now the Apostle is calling *us* by those same titles. Isn't that amazing?"

"Of course, it's amazing," replied Hannah, "it's God's grace-amazing grace! 'Giving us something we didn't deserve and could not earn'; that's what grace means, doesn't it?"

One of the Elders intervened: "Are we going to have a general discussion now, or are we going hear what the Apostle has written?" he asked. "I suggest that we can meet later in the week, in smaller groups, to discuss all the questions that we have." "That's a very good idea," agreed a second Elder, "but for now let's just listen to the letter."

# CHAPTER 1

# Holiness and Grace

### READ: COLOSSIANS 1: 1–14.

### EXPLORE:

i. *Paul refers to the people in Colossae as "holy" ("saints") and he means it. To what extent do we see that as applying to our Church/ Fellowship today? How does each of us share and show God's "grace and peace" (v.1)?*

ii. *The Apostle found God's people in Colossae attractive because of their "faith . . . love . . . and hope" (vv. 3–5); what do I see as most attractive about the church I attend, or Christians I have met?*

iii. *Paul prays that God's people in Colossae would be filled with "the knowledge of God's will and with all the wisdom and understanding that God's Spirit gives" (v.9). What difference would it make to the church/fellowship that I attend if this prayer was answered for us today and what else would we ask God for on behalf of our worship community?*

iv. *The Apostle shows how God's grace can make the people in Colossae productive: "Your lives will produce all kinds of good deeds; you will be made strong with all the strength that comes from God's glorious power" (v.10)*. What "fruit" should we each like to see growing in us personally and in the fellowship at your church?

v. The Apostle ends this section by inviting his hearers to be reflective, thinking about the inheritance they are to receive and their experience of transition from the *"powers of darkness to the kingdom of the Son; and from condemnation to forgiveness" (vv. 11–12)*. How would you describe the difference that knowing Christ and seeking to follow him is making in your life?

## DRAWING TOGETHER

Letter-writing is a dying art. Apart from a few stalwarts who diligently keep sending letters and cards, most of us have resorted to emails and text-messages, where the rule is, keep it brief; keep it simple. But there are certain times and some themes where a text message will not do; and there is still something special about receiving a hand-written note on a special occasion.

So, imagine how the Christians in Colossae felt as their reader unrolled the scroll of the Apostle's letter and they heard for the very first time the words that he had taken the trouble to put together for them from his prison house in Rome.

At one level, it is a very ordinary letter. Just as we used until recently to begin our letters, "My Dear Friend, how are you?" So, the Apostle begins in a quite standard way for his time with a "Greeting". (I learned while in South Africa, and in my contacts with members from other countries in Africa, the importance of greeting "properly," not in the cursory western way!) But what a Greeting this was: from an "Apostle," someone who has been chosen and sent out by God; to "saints" the people of God in a specific place.

As we read the words of the Apostle, so many centuries later, what are the things that we notice? As a Church, how would we answer the question, "How are you?"

The letter suggests three sub-headings that we might use to help us reach an answer: Attractive, Productive and Reflective.

## Attractive

The first qualities that the Apostle mentions, and that we might look for, are ones that make the church attractive.

Col 1:3, "In our prayers for you we always thank God, the Father of our Lord Jesus Christ, 4 for we have heard of your *faith* in Christ Jesus, and of the *love* that you have for all the saints, 5 because of the *hope* laid up for you in heaven."

*Faith in Christ Jesus*. That means, trusting that what he says is true–that the picture he presents of God and of humanity is *authentic* and *authoritative*; and it means reliance on Christ—knowing that we cannot make it on our own and therefore depending on him for the strength to live lives that are in line with our calling as saints.

*Love for all God's people*. Having goodwill towards, and benevolence for, each and every member of God's family; treating them as if they were truly part of me, because in Christ they are.

*Hope laid up in heaven*. The Christians in Colossae lived as if they knew what life was about; their hope was not mere wishful thinking about "pie in the sky by and by when I die"; their hope was a copper-bottomed, gilt-edged security about the purpose of God that gave them assurance and confidence for each trial each day. They were assured that all would be well, and that all manner of things would be well.

The reports that Paul received described an Attractive church; one where they had grasped the fundamentals of the Christian way and lived according to the basic trilogy that was also commended to the Church in Corinth—faith, hope, love.

So, what of our church: if the Apostle asked for a report on our faith-hope-love rating, how would we score? What evidence could we offer of the strength of our faith, the scope of our love, and the steadfastness of our hope—and here's the thing, do we have a longing to be better–to grow in grace and holiness? Dear Friends, how are you?

## Productive

The Church in Colossae could be described not only as Attractive, but also as, productive.

Col 1: 6, "Just as [the gospel] is bearing fruit and growing in the whole world, so it has been bearing fruit among yourselves from the day you heard it and truly comprehended the grace of God."

So, according to Colossians, what is the secret of being a productive church? The Apostle suggests three requirements:

*Comprehending the grace of God.* (Col 1:6.) Understanding and embracing what "grace" means. Not just knowing *about* grace, but entering fully into the ocean of God's grace, being overwhelmed, swamped, drowned in God's grace; becoming aware at first hand of just how loving, forgiving, accepting, unpredictably risk-taking God is. That was what the Church in Colossae learned from their area Presbyter, Epaphras, says the Apostle Paul. He spent time agonising over you in prayer (wrestling in prayer, like Jacob with the Angel at Peniel) and would not get up from his knees until he knew that God had answered his prayer that his friends in Colossae would all be filled with all the grace of God.

*Filled with all the grace of God*, or to put it another way, as in Col 1:8, having "love in the Spirit." Spiritual productivity comes from the overflow of God's Spirit in us; we cannot just make ourselves more loving, it is the Spirit of love who makes it possible for us to love. Productivity comes when we have the Spirit of God within us, teaching us to comprehend and transmit the immeasurable grace of God.

*Continuing in the grace of God.* Christian living is not about an initial spurt followed by long inertia. Christianity is not a vaccination that we are given at Baptism or Confirmation that keeps us "protected" for the rest of our lives and even for eternity. Being a follower of Christ is about becoming more and more like Christ; not just comprehending the grace of God but continuing in that grace.

Holiness is a gift of grace. It comes from our connectedness with God and the people of God, and one of the most obvious and most effective ways of tapping into that grace is through prayer.

The Apostle recognises that, and so he says in Colossians 1: 9–12, "We have not ceased praying for you and asking that you may be *filled with the knowledge of God's will* in all spiritual wisdom and understanding, so that you may *lead lives worthy of the Lord*, as you bear fruit in every good work and as you grow in the knowledge of God. May you *be strong* with all the strength that comes from God's glorious power, and may you be *prepared to endure everything with patience,* while *joyfully giving thanks* to the Father who has enabled you to share in the inheritance of the saints in light."

These verses make clear the aim of the believer, which is, "to lead lives worthy of the Lord and to bear fruit in all kinds of good works" (v. 10); and, also, what is needed in order to fulfil that aim, namely, "spiritual wisdom and understanding," or to be "filled with the knowledge of God's will (v. 9)."

This is nothing less than a prayer for holiness; that which John Wesley described as the "second blessing," following on from, and building on, our experience of God's grace that gave a new direction to, and focus for, our lives. That grace makes it possible for us to:

- Increase in our knowledge of God's will until we are full of that knowledge;
- be strong, with a strength that comes directly from the glorious energy of God, and flows into that part of our being where our will, or resolve, our conscience and our ambitions spring from;
- have a hope, that enables us to go through life, not with grim determination and gritted teeth, but with joyful perseverance and enduring thankfulness—"be prepared to endure everything with patience, while *joyfully* giving thanks to the Father who has enabled you to share in the inheritance of the saints in light."

Now that's what I call productive living!

So, at the start of the letter, the Apostle asks, "Dear Friends, how are you?" It is a question to "saints" about their holiness given by grace: Are we Attractive as a Church? Are we Productive as Christians?

## Reflective

And perhaps there is just one final question from these opening verses of Colossians 1: to what extent are we *reflective*? How much, and how deeply do we think about where we have come from, and about our present relationship with God?

Paul uses the language and imagery of war and of slavery to describe the spiritual experience of the church in Colossae. Col 1: 13, "[The Father] has *rescued* us from the power of darkness and transferred us into the kingdom of his beloved Son, in whom we have *redemption*, the *forgiveness of sins*."

Rescued; redeemed; forgiven: is that our testimony here in this church?

- That we were lost, in danger, away from God, and God took the initiative, made a plan to rescue us and bring us home;

- That we were, in effect, slaves–controlled by powers we couldn't get away from, doing things that we didn't even want to do and that we knew would make us less wholesome and less human, and through the death of God's Son a way was found of redeeming us, buying us back, of satisfying the bloodlust that overshadows our world;

- Or that, quite simply, we found that all the wrongdoing that had built up on our slate was one day wiped clean, as we came to God, admitted our failures and weakness, asked God's forgiveness and resolved that with the help of God we would turn away from our self-centred living and follow the way of Christ.

Rescued, redeemed, forgiven: does any of that ring true for you?

Dear Friends, how are you? This can be the day, when because of what God has done in Christ, we can know and we can say, like those first Christians in Colossae, "By God's grace, we are well; being made whole by the holiness of God." Amen.

## A PRAYER:

*Splendour beyond imagining, brightness beyond compare, power that never runs out and never pollutes or corrupts, all flowing from infinite love: God, of your grace you offer this holiness to us for our cleansing, our healing, our renewing. With joy and thanksgiving, we open ourselves to you, inviting you to be the centre of our lives. Amen.*

# CHAPTER 2

# Christ and Holiness

### READ: COLOSSIANS 1:15–2:5

### EXPLORE:

i. *"Christ is the image of the invisible God." (v.15)*: What is it about God that Jesus helps you to see more clearly?
ii. *"In [or 'by'] Christ all things . . . were created" (v.16)*: As you read these words and look also at John 1: 3, how does this influence the way that you worship Christ?
iii. *"In him all the fullness of God was pleased to dwell" (v. 20)*: Which aspects of the fullness of God do you most desire for yourself—and for your church?
iv. *"The mystery that has been hidden . . . has now been revealed . . . which is, Christ in you, the hope of glory" (vv. 26–27)*: how assured are you that Christ is in you and how does that influence your approach to life?
v. The Apostle's aim was to *"present everyone mature in Christ" (v. 28)*: In which areas do you see yourself as still needing to grow most, and who helps you as you continue to learn?

## DRAWING TOGETHER

Dymphna, one of the younger members of the Church in Colossae, was wrestling with a problem. (No, not the man in her life, this time—though she did hope that the Apostle's letter would say something that would help her on that front.) Dymphna's struggle was with trying to place Jesus in the hierarchy of deities and rulers that she had heard about.

Before becoming a follower of the Jesus Way, Dymphna had been part of a group in Colossae that taught her that the world was dominated and controlled by all sorts of spiritual forces; some of them were benign and friendly, others were much more mischievous and even malevolent: you wouldn't want to get on the wrong side of them, or you never know what might happen. Dymphna would check her astrological readings regularly, to give her some clues as to how she should behave.

What Dymphna wanted to know was how Jesus, the Messiah, the Special Chosen One, fitted into this hierarchy of Powers and Rulers, Angels and Potentates. She listened carefully and didn't have to wait long before she was offered a way of thinking about the place of Jesus and how he could help with her longing to be connected.

## Cosmos

Starting with the big picture, the Apostle proposed that Jesus was to be seen as *The Image of the invisible God* (Col 1: 15a.)

If you want to know what the Creator, the origin and source of all things is like, look at Jesus, said the Apostle. Believe and trust that the picture that Jesus paints is the true one; that it is authoritative and authentic.

Dymphna thought about the accounts that she had been hearing of the teachings of Jesus: that God cared even for the sparrow that gets thrown in for free when you buy a pair, and that human beings rate much more highly in God's scheme than sparrows; that God is the farmer that cares so much for the fate of every sheep that he values one that is lost just as much as ninety-nine that are safe; that God is like a father who waits and watches patiently, longingly, endlessly, for the son who packed up and left because he wanted to "do his own thing." Being the Image of God, Jesus helped to make the invisible God visible.

It was this picture that Dymphna decided to trust. She was content that others should rely on other glimpses of the inexhaustible fullness of God, and she knew that some of these would enrich her own understanding; but in Christ she saw a revelation of God that made sense for her, and that inspired her and fulfilled her deepest longings for holiness and connectedness.

The Apostle went on to present Jesus as *The Initial Outflow* (Col 1:15 b). "He is the first born of creation," not separate from God, distinct from God as the rest of creation, but an expression of God—"begotten, not made," says our Creed. The picture is of God becoming so full within the divine be-ing that there had to be some overflow, and the overflow had all the characteristics and personality (or rather, "Godsonality") of God. Think of jam-making and the continuous heat causing the mixture to boil over: that overspill is Jesus, truly God; part of the original mixture.

And there was a further way of thinking of Jesus on the cosmic scale, namely, as: *The Instrument* (Col 1: 16). "In Christ and through Christ, was created everything that has been created." God, having "overflowed", uses that divine manifestation (variously called the Word, the Logos, the Reason and the Wisdom of God) to shape and fashion the divine energy and bring all the rest of creation into being. Perhaps the analogy here is not jam-making, but the overflow of lava from a volcano, which over time becomes weathered and transformed into a fertile landscape. The overflowing mixture of God's creative energy and being crystalizes out into stars and planets, earthworms and earwigs, grasshoppers, giraffes—and human beings.

Dymphna sat in stunned silence. She had her answer: Jesus was not a god to be worshipped alongside other deities of a pantheon; Jesus was the Christ, the Chosen One, through whom everything else came to be.

But the Apostle was still not finished with his placing of Jesus in the Cosmos, he also showed Jesus as *The Integrator* (Col 1:16b-17). "In him all things hold together." He is the gravity, not just for earth or planets and solar systems, but of the whole universe, things visible and invisible. All things were created through him and for him, and all things find their place and fit together under his gravitational pull.

Speaking some time ago to a Professor from one of our Universities, I couldn't help sharing the sense of wonder and excitement he expressed as he described his work with an electron microscope. A whole new world has been opened to us with the invention of this instrument.

Or again, as I watch programmes about the stars and the planets and followed the developments in the placing of telescopes in South Africa as part of an international project of space observation, I got a real buzz, a feeling of wonder and excitement—there was so much yet to discover and to explore–galaxies, supernova; unlimited, inexhaustible realms. And all of it, and much more besides, owes to Christ its origin and finds its integration only through Christ; Christ is the one by whom and for whom everything was created, and Christ is the one that holds it all together.

Who is Christ for us? Whether in Colossae, or in Cape Town, Croydon or Chicago, this is part of our Creed: that we connect with the Holy God, as we accept Christ as Image, Initial Outflow, Instrument, and the Integrator–far, far, more significant than we might have imagined; truly a Cosmic Christ.

Not content to leave Christ "out in space," the Apostle goes on to show who Christ is relation to the gathering of people in a particular place, even one as seemingly insignificant as Colossae.

## Church

And here also we are offered different perspectives:

*The Foremost Feature* "He is the head of the body, the church;" (Col 1: 18a). The Church claims that it is led and controlled by Christ, its Head, which means that when people look at the Church, they should be able to see the features of Christ in us and recognise him in us and through us. We can all put together our own list of the characteristics of Christ and then ask ourselves just how faithfully and fully our own fellowship displays those features.

*The Front Runner* "He is the beginning, the firstborn from the dead," (Col 1:18b). He has been around the track of life; ran the perfect race, and was awarded the winner's medal, resurrection life; life eternal and complete. But this was not intended as a unique achievement, it was a demonstration and stimulation for every believer. It is as if Jesus is saying to each one of us: "You can do this too; attaining the prize is a possibility for you as well. It doesn't depend on your state of fitness, the length and complexity of your training, but on your connecting with me, sticking with me and drawing your strength for each step of the race from me. Because I live, you are going to live as well."

*The Fountainhead* "In him all the fullness of God was pleased to dwell;" (Col 1:19). What an amazing thought that is! It sounds unthinkable, impossible. But perhaps what the Apostle has in mind is not the scale of Deity, but rather, the sample: a bucket of water drawn from the Atlantic Ocean will have the same chemical composition as the Atlantic from which it is drawn, all the essential properties. In the same way, in Christ we have all the essential properties of God-ness that we can comprehend and relate to as human beings, and we are offered those qualities in a ceaseless outflow through Jesus Christ—an abundance symbolised by the plentiful supply of wine in the first miracle that he performed.

*The Friend-Maker* Col 1:20, "Through him God was pleased to reconcile all things to God's very being, whether in earth or in heaven, by making peace through the blood of the cross." Dying on the cross, Christ shows the full extent of God's love for all humanity and extends God's "right hand" of acceptance and friendship to us. It is through clasping that hand in faith, that our hostility dissolves and we are transformed from enemies into friends and family members.

*The Focus-Giver* Strange teachings were abroad in Colossae and strange combinations of insights were being promoted. It was inevitable, therefore, that the followers of a new Way struggled to work out how it related to their previous beliefs and the convictions of their friends and family members.

The Apostle was only too aware of how easy it was for these early followers of Christ in Colossae to become distracted and confused, and then to forget what their life in Christ was all about. So, he reminds them of their history and of their destiny: "You who were once estranged and hostile in mind, doing evil deeds, he has now reconciled . . . so as to present you *holy* and *blameless* and *irreproachable* before him–provided that you continue securely established and steadfast in the faith, without shifting from the hope promised by the gospel that you heard," (Col 2: 21–23).

When life seems purposeless, we are called to remember the gospel, which tells how the purposes of God were not thwarted by the resistance and rejection of the religious and political powers of the day: that is hope. When we lose sight of what Church is about, Christ is there to point us in the right direction, the direction that is illuminated by the light coming from his cross: that is hope; and it is on hope that we build our steadfastness. Christ helps us to re-focus.

Who is Christ for us? Who do we need him to be today, not in abstract philosophical or cosmic terms, but for us personally as a follower of the way or a seeker after truth and holiness and fullness of life?

- Do we truly accept him as Head, "the Boss"? And what a Boss he can be: the kind of Boss who stoops and washes the smelly feet of those who need his service.

- Is he our front-runner, our pacesetter? In the race of life how are we going to find the energy and the endurance to finish well and gain the prize of holiness, life eternal?

- Have we experienced the renewing and refreshing that comes through having Christ as our Fountainhead, our personal access-point and 'hole in the wall' through which you can draw on the limitless resources of God?

- Have we found him to be the Friend-maker, the one who takes us to the Godhead, introduces us with an arm around our shoulder and invites us to sit at table and stay forever in the home that he prepared for each of us?

- Is Christ for us the Focus-Giver, the one who helps us to make sense of the chaos that threatens to overwhelm us?

Who is Jesus for us, in the setting of the Church, as well as in the scheme of Creation?

But perhaps the biggest challenge by far for us will be to decide how we respond to the call of Christ and weigh the demands of Christ.

## Commitment.

Let's be clear about this, we all make commitments: commitments to those we love; commitments to our employers or colleagues; commitments to clubs and groups; commitments to ourselves. The question is then, how does our commitment to Christ and holiness relate to these other commitments?

We do not have to go far into the Gospels to recognise how radical, how deep, how total, is the commitment that Jesus expected of those who were to be his disciples. Whether we use the kind of scales that shows the weight, or one that gives a value from one to ten, or one to a hundred, Christ is looking for a commitment that outranks, outweighs and out-measures *all* our other commitments.

Christ must be *The Pinnacle* of our Commitments.

The Apostle puts forward different pictures of how our commitment to Christ might be expressed: For some people it might mean being *Sent out in Christ's Service*.

Paul described himself as "a servant of the Gospel;" (Col 1: 23). Or let us not soften the requirement: this is not about acting as a civil servant; the Apostle refers to himself as a "slave" for the Gospel–someone who, every minute of every day is, if not "on duty", at least "on call"; someone whose very existence is subject to the will of a master; someone without rights, only responsibilities. But what caused the Apostle to see himself in this way, was not a sense of guilt or fear, it was an all-consuming passion to share the good news.

For other Christians, commitment might involve *Speaking of Christ's Salvation*. Paul knew that in Colossae there were particular sects, Gnostics, who claimed that it was through special knowledge and having secret passwords (which only the Gnostics knew) that the chosen ones would find the salvation they were looking for. The Apostle was passionately opposed to such a teaching wherever it occurred, and he was prepared to travel far and wide, as committed as a slave sent on a mission by an owner, to let people know that the secret was out, and the mystery was no longer concealed: their hope of glory lay in having Christ in them (Col 1:27).

Christ's commission is to all of us: "Go, tell." We show our commitment as we speak of Christ's salvation.

And for yet others of us, the commitment required might be, *Sharing Christ's Suffering*. Paul's testimony from prison was, (Col 1:24): "In my flesh I am completing what is lacking in Christ's afflictions, for the sake of his body, the Church." In 2 Corinthians 11: 24–29, under provocation, the Apostle describes graphically how he suffered shipwreck, beatings, imprisonment, sleeplessness, blazing rows–all so that he could "make the word of God fully known;" (Col 1: 25).

I wonder what are the stories of personal commitment and sacrifice that have inspired you most: accounts of people who devoted their lives to studying one particular species, enduring hunger and taking risks that we might better understand the life of the wolf or the shark, the tiger or the sloth? People who stood against tyrannical regimes and were willing to face imprisonment or death rather than keep silent? People who left their family and homeland and became aliens in another country, serving the least and lowliest there because they were driven, constrained, by love?

If our commitment was being weighed or measured today, what would the scales show? The good news is that we do not have to be despondent if we think that we are not showing the measure of commitment that we should like to. It was something that took time for the closest followers of Jesus—and look at the head start that they had!

Like those first disciples, we can find that Christ not only asks us to make him the *Pinnacle* of commitment; he offers to those who seek, *The Power* for our Commitment.

It is that power, "Christ in us," that makes it possible for us, *To Show Christ's Splendour*. "It is [Christ] whom we proclaim . . .

warning... and teaching... so that we may present everyone mature in Christ." (Col 1:28)

The ultimate test of commitment is the closeness of our likeness to Christ—having Christ in us. The challenge is to experience God's grace in such a way that what is seen is not our sacrifice or commitment, but the "glory" of Christ.

The Apostle makes clear that it is not something that we can achieve on our own, so he opens a further option for us, which is, *To Struggle on behalf of Christ's Saints.* "I toil and struggle with all the energy that [Christ] powerfully inspires in me. I want you to know how much I am struggling for you and for those in Laodicea, and for all who have not seen me face to face." (Col 1:29–2:1).

The Apostle's struggle (hard work) has a double aim, to encourage and to enlighten: "I want their hearts to be encouraged and united in love, so that they may have all the riches of assured understanding and have the knowledge of God's mystery, that is, Christ himself, in whom are hid all the treasures of wisdom and knowledge." (Col 2:1–3a)

What a difference it would make to our fellowship if we could know that our sisters and brothers were praying for us regularly and unremittingly, that we might be encouraged in our commitment and have the wisdom to know how to follow Christ more faithfully.

It is when we see who Christ really is that all of this becomes possible: seeing him in the Scheme of Creation and the Society of the Church, but most of all in the Scales of our Commitment; the Christ who is Holiness embodied.

## A PRAYER

*When we were stumbling around in the dark, confused by different voices, you came to us, O Christ: showing your love, bringing our spirits to life, shedding light on our path, connecting us to the very source of life—eternal holiness. Christ, our connector, infused with holiness, we offer ourselves to be transformed by you, re-made by you, and to know the blessing of sharing your glory that you willed for us from all eternity. Amen.*

# CHAPTER 3
# Holiness and Rules

### READ: COLOSSIANS 2:6-23.

### EXPLORE:

i. *Paul uses different images in 2:7 to describe our spiritual growth, "rooted... built up... strengthened... over-flowing..."—how do you relate your own spiritual life to each of these pictures?*
ii. *What examples of "human traditions," or teachings about the "ruling spirits of the universe" have you come across, which are offered as additions to faith in Christ, and how does Paul's teaching about "fullness in Christ" (v.10) help us deal with such ideas?*
iii. *What do you see as some of the most basic needs that humans have, and what do we learn from Col 2: 11–15 about the way that Christ meets those needs?*
iv. *Why might one find the addition of rules quite appealing as we follow Christ (vv. 16–18, 21), and what are the dangers in following such rules?*
v. *Which rules of your church fellowship do you personally find most "challenging," and which do you see as creating difficulties in relation to your witness to the wider community?*

vi. *Paul mentions "Giving thanks" repeatedly (1:3; 1:12; 2:7; 3:17): What are the things that you have through your relationship with Christ for which you can give thanks to God?*

## DRAWING TOGETHER

Caleb, another member of the gathering in Colossae, also had some questions: he was terrified of doing the wrong thing. He spent his whole life memorising all the requirements of the Jewish Law–not just the 'Ten Commandments' of Sinai, but all the 613 regulations that the Rabbis had developed beyond them and that the Scribes had re-iterated and re-interpreted.

Caleb wanted Salvation–peace and fullness of life–and the only way he knew of achieving that was by keeping the rules, faithfully and fully. So, Caleb was quick to follow all the latest dos and don'ts that went around Colossae. He was also trying to understand the rules of being a follower of Jesus.

Caleb listened closely as the letter from Paul was read and thought carefully about what it all meant. Suddenly it was as if a flash of inspiration blazed in his mind and he decided that there were three simple tests that he would apply to all rules and regulations from then on, and he was sure that this would help him become more connected to God and to the people around him.

## Test of Authoritativeness

If anyone puts forward a law or rule that they claim I should follow, thought Caleb, I will ask myself, "Who is saying this? What authority is there for this rule?"

Caleb decided on this test when he heard the Apostle's words (Col 2:8, 9) "The full content of the divine nature lives in Christ... he is supreme over every spiritual ruler and authority."

Caleb realised that he did not need a long list of rules, or a detailed breakdown of all the dos and don'ts, what he needed was to be in union with Christ in the company of Christ's followers.

It was clear from the Apostle's words that Christ would have greater authority than *Customs and Traditions*. Christ had challenged the religious people of his day for giving greater weight to "the tradition of the Elders" than to God's desire that they show compassion and mercy.

Christ's authority should also outweigh the dictates of *Contemporary Trends and Fashions*. Caleb thought about the whole hierarchy of spiritual rulers that he had discussed with Dymphna, and he realised that if Christ was indeed the one who revealed the inmost and essential character of God, the one who made known the thoughts and intentions of God, then no other authority should be allowed to take precedence.

I wonder how we would fare if we applied Caleb's test of Authoritativeness to our lives: the rules that we follow (or choose to ignore) do they have upon them the stamp of the authority of Christ? Do we give more weight to "Popular Culture", New Age Spirituality, Political Ideology, than we do to thinking that has its roots in the mind and the teaching of Christ?

Caleb realised that alongside the test of Authoritativeness, it would be right to have a second test.

## Test of Inclusiveness

As he struggled to learn the requirements of the Law so that he might fulfil them, Caleb had often wondered about the words of the Prophet Jeremiah, "I will put my Law within them and write it on their hearts . . . No longer shall they teach one another or say to each other, 'Know the Lord', for they will all know me," (Jeremiah 31:31, 33).

Caleb had often wished that God's Law could be, not so much a set of rules that he had to follow to curb and restrain his personal desires, but rather a spontaneous expression of the kind of person that he was.

He saw the Test of Inclusiveness as being about the capacity to, *Experience God's Law Inwardly*. The Apostle seemed to be opening up that possibility: "In union with Christ . . . you have been freed from the power of the sinful self . . . you were spiritually dead, but God has brought you to life with Christ." (Col 2:11).

It was having Christ within that would make it possible both to know and to do the will of God. The Test of Inclusiveness was then to discern how any law, any rule, arose from and related to the life of Christ within the people of Christ.

Inclusiveness would also mean, *Extending God's Life Outwardly*. The rules that mattered, Caleb saw, were the ones that made it possible for others to catch a glimpse of the fullness of life, the holiness, that God was offering to everyone.

He thought about all the rules governing what he could and could not do on the Sabbath; all the rules about clean and unclean foods; about what do with bodily emissions; rules for every aspect of life. He had to admit that they did not have about them the feel of a life full and over-flowing. They were, in any case, rules that only the privileged few would stand any chance of being able to fulfil, and well beyond the reach of most people in Colossae; they were for an exclusive group, an elite of specially chosen people, and the rest were automatically excluded from salvation, according to the old way of thinking.

Now the Apostle was saying that something else was on offer in Christ: "The full content of divine nature lives in Christ, in his humanity, and you have been given full life in union with Christ." (Col 2: 9, 10). Caleb resolved that he would not give house room any longer to any rule that would deny, diminish, or get in the way of the fullness of life that he had been given in Christ. That was to be his test of Inclusiveness: can this be part of Christ in me, and can others be brought into this experience also?

That led Caleb to his third test:

## Test of Effectiveness

He would ask about the outcome that the proffered rules would have in people's lives. In particular he would ask if there was effectiveness *In Personal Formation*. What kind of person will I, or other people, become by following this rule?

## Holiness and Rules

The Apostle warned, "Make sure that no one enslaves you by means of the worthless deceit of human wisdom." (Col 2:8). And again (in Col 2:18), "Do not allow yourselves to be condemned by anyone who claims to be superior because of special visions, or who insists on false humility and the worship of angels."

He was writing about the threats faced by Christians in Colossae in his day, and we could compile our own profile of teachings and outlooks in our day that are about enslaving and condemning. A rule that turns people into slaves of an institution or unthinking automatons completely subject to the "authorities", will not lead to the fulfilment for which human beings were created and which in this life we are intended to grow towards.

We are to remember that "It is for freedom that Christ has liberated us" and having been freed from the slavery of sin, we should not fall or be pushed into the slavery of sanctimonious-ness. Ask about effectiveness in Personal Formation: will this make me a more Christ-like person?

Then ask about effectiveness, *In Spiritual Fruit-bearing*. The key message is found in Col 2:6, "Since you have accepted Christ Jesus as Lord, live in union with him." In the following verse, we are then given a series of pictures and metaphors of what that means:

*Cultivation.* "Keep your roots deep in him." Christ is the fertile soil from whom you will draw the nutrients you need and who will keep you steady even when strong winds are blowing.

*Construction.* "Build your lives upon him." Christ is the foundation on which each course of the brickwork of our lives must rest. We recognise that sometimes the building goes up very slowly according to the resources are available.

*Consolidation.* "Become stronger in your faith." Bodybuilding is becoming more and more popular, and what is being recognised increasingly is both the importance using muscles, and of using them in the right way. I sometimes think that we need body-building classes to help Christians keep their spiritual muscles toned: faith becomes firmer as it is exercised; hope increases in its capacity for movement, and love becomes stronger.

*Celebration.* "Be filled and overflow with thanksgiving." In his letter to the Galatians, the Apostle lists joy as one of the fruits of the

Spirit. (Gal 5:22). A life of rules can often become a life without joy and that shows incomplete fruit bearing and hinders our spiritual fulfilment. In Colossians the Apostle encourages the sense of joy as he draws attention repeatedly to all that God has done for us and who Christ is for us.

So, whose rules have we been living by, and what has been their effect in our lives?

"The full content of divine nature lives in Christ and we have been given full life in union with him."

Let us make sure that we live lives that, when tested, are true to that testimony; lives ruled by the holiness that connects us to God and to our neighbour.

## A PRAYER

*Lord, let your holiness be like the gravity that keeps us connected to the earth, but does not chain us; like the pull of the sun that keeps the planets of our solar system in their paths across the trackless expanse of space; so, may we live lives that are ordered, and in that order may we find our freedom. Amen.*

## CHAPTER 4

# At Peace in Holiness

**READ: COLOSSIANS 3: 1-17**

**EXPLORE:**

i. Can you recall "setting your heart" on something, either as a child or more recently? How did you feel as you thought about that thing? What did you do to help make your longing come true?
ii. Where does your mind "drift off to" when you are on your own and you do not have to focus on something particular? What does Paul suggest as a focus for the Christian's thoughts and what reasons does he give for that focus?
iii. Which of the "clothes" that Paul tells us to take off (3:5–11) would our culture encourage us to keep wearing?
iv. Paul describes the Christians in Colossae as "God's chosen ones, holy and beloved" (3:12): how do you picture someone who is described in this way? Which of the "clothes" that Paul recommends do you find missing from your wardrobe?
v. What are the steps that Paul urges Christians to take when there are disputes and grievances in the church? How far could this apply in the wider society?

vi. *How could the worship in your local fellowship be developed further to bring you closer to the pattern Paul describes in Col. 3:16–17?*

## DRAWING TOGETHER

Dolores and Dimitri breathed a huge sigh of relief when Caleb told them how, based on what he heard in Paul's letter, he had settled on three tests to help him decide whether or not he should follow a particular rule that someone else was putting forward. The Test of Authoritativeness—where did the rule come from? The Test of Inclusiveness—could it be internalised and help others to enter God's Kingdom? The Test of Effectiveness—would the proposed rule help him to be more like Christ, the Master?

Dolores and Dimitri liked Caleb's scheme because they had both been struggling to avoid the straitjacket of legalism on the one hand, and the seduction of libertarianism on the other. At one time they had even thought about adopting the strict rules of the Ascetics with all their fasting and penance, but they had quickly decided that was not for them.

Caleb's tests were helpful, but still not quite sufficient. They listened more closely to what the Apostle had written, and there in the third section of his letter, they found their answer: "The peace of Christ is to guide you in the decisions you make; for it is to this peace that God has called you together in one body." (Col 3:15).

They thought about what their aims should be as they set out in life together; about the kind of people that they wanted to be; and how their character would be reflected in their conduct. As they considered each possibility, they waited for that inner peace that they knew would come when their thoughts and desires were in tune with the will and purpose of their Master.

## Being Connected

Dolores and Dimitri were clear that through Christ they were being offered a way of being in close relationship with God and with their fellow believers. They were being connected *Spiritually* for living. "You have been raised to life with Christ, so set your hearts on heavenly (that is 'spiritual', 'eternal') things. Keep your mind fixed on things there, not on things of this earth." (Col 3:1, 2 GNB).

Heart and mind; ambition and attention: it was as if a new dimension, a new source of energy, had opened up in their lives; they were sure that there was more to life than the physical and material; and their goal was clear—to gain the full realization of the life they had begun to experience in part already. "Your real life is Christ and when he appears, then you too will appear with him and share his glory." (Col 3:4, GNB). There was no doubt in the minds of Dolores and Dimitri about what their goal was in life; they were Connected *Spiritually*.

And they found too that they were connected *Socially*. Being connected to Christ meant that they were also connected to everyone else who was similarly connected to Christ. They were part of a rich and diverse family: "There is no longer any distinction between Gentiles and Jews, circumcised and uncircumcised, barbarians, savages, slaves and free people, but Christ is all, Christ is in all." (Col 3:11).

Dolores and Dimitri couldn't help smiling as they looked around at all the people crammed into the home of Philemon and Apphia: this was Christ's body in all its richness, and they felt the peace of being at home–connected.

Just as they were getting used to that idea and savouring the peace that it brought, they found that the Apostle had changed tack in his letter and was talking about clothes . . . Clothes?!

## Being Clothed

Dolores found her mind wandering for a moment. She tried to remember whether it was last week, or the week before, that Dimitri had looked at the dress she had spent ages choosing and had asked in a studiedly casual sort of way, 'Were you thinking of wearing that when we visit my parents later today?' Clothes: definitely a touchy subject.

She re-focused on what the Apostle was saying, as he pointed to the *Contrasts* that he wanted them to be aware of.

It was a powerful message. Think of your old way of life as a set of clothes that you used to wear, and which were as polluted as if you had fallen into one of the open sewers of Colossae with them. "Get rid of those feelings of resentment and those outbursts of blazing temper," he said; "burn the dirty clothes of hatred, cursing people, and dirty talk. Because you have taken off the old self, the old clothes must go as well. You have put on a new self. This is the new being which God, its Creator, is constantly renewing in God's own likeness, in order to bring you into a full knowledge of God's own being."

The Apostle continued with the analogy and went on painting the picture: "You are the people of God; whom God loved and chose for divine ownership. So then, you must clothe yourself with compassion, kindness, humility, gentleness and patience."

Dolores felt as if she was standing in front of an open wardrobe and Christ was handing her one garment after another, saying, "Try this one; it's just the right size for you; it will fit perfectly, and I think that you will feel really good wearing this." She looked at each one in turn; what a selection there was!

She glanced across at Dimitri and noticed that there was a look of real peace on his face as he listened to this section of the letter. Perhaps she could use the Apostle's words later to start a conversation about clothes!

As she listened further, she recognised that she needed to be aware of not just the *Contrasts*, but also the *Completing* of her attire.

The most-costly, and the most necessary garments had been put towards the end of the rail: forgiveness—so vital for those times when you feel that people have been tugging at all the rest of the garments and they are getting frayed. And then, "When you think that you need a finishing touch, this is the very thing: put on this garment of divine love; (Agape; God's unconquerable benevolence) it will make your outfit *perfect*."

Dolores was at peace; she had found the right clothes to go with her new life. She knew the peace of being connected and of being clothed and already she felt she had taken a major step forward in her search for life that was whole and integrated.

But the Apostle had one further dimension of Peace still to offer:

## Being Christ-filled

Col. 3:16, "Christ's message in all its richness must live in your hearts. Teach and instruct each other with all wisdom." Dolores saw that if she was going to continue experiencing the deep peace that she had found, there would have to be attention to *Sound Teaching*.

There were so many doctrines, so many voices, it was all too easy to lose one's way; it was also tempting sometimes simply to take teaching without testing whether or not it was sound: whether it was in line with the Apostolic faith that had been handed down and in keeping with the insights and wisdom of the living community of faith. Sound teaching was one of the requirements for being Christ-filled.

But the Apostle urged that having the peace of being Christ-filled would also be expressed in *Shared Thanksgiving*. "Sing psalms, hymns and sacred songs; sing to God with thanksgiving in your hearts." Dimitri thought about how critical he had become about some of the old psalms that they used in their worship gatherings and how others had spoken against the new songs that had been introduced. Now he asked himself, what is the focus of our singing? Why do we sing? Was it really an offering of praise to God, or mostly for our own satisfaction?

According to the Apostle, singing in thankfulness was an expression and extension of living in thankfulness: "Everything you say or do should be done in the name of the Lord Jesus (as if you are doing it for the Master) and through him show your thankfulness to our Creator God, the Father."

"The peace that Christ gives is to be your guide (your umpire) in all the decisions you make." May the Peace of the Lord be always with you, as you live in the holiness of God. Amen.

## A PRAYER

*Peace, Lord; not an escape from trouble, but the ability to sleep even while the storm is raging; not the unstable stillness of suppression, but the letting go of tension, sinking into the depths of your eternal, life-restoring peace, knowing that underneath us are your everlasting arms. Grant us peace. Amen.*

## CHAPTER 5
# Holiness: Debits and Credits

### READ: COLOSSIANS 3: 18-4:1.

### EXPLORE:

i. *It is instinctive for humans to put more emphasis on getting what they are entitled to receive, rather than on fulfilling their responsibilities/paying their dues: what motivation does the Christian have for reversing this order?*
ii. *What are the main challenges you find today to the guidelines for husband-wife relationships that Paul sets out in Col 3:18–19?*
iii. *Look back at Col 3:12–17; how does this passage help as we seek to fulfil the obligations of Col 3:18–21?*
iv. *Parent-child relationships can be difficult: what part does "obedience" play in such relationships, and what attitudes or actions on the part of parents might lead to children becoming "discouraged and embittered"?*
v. *What connections do you see between what Paul says about slave-master relationships (3:22—4:1) and the work situation in this country today?*

## DRAWING TOGETHER

Philemon was feeling both inspired and relaxed as he sat and listened to Paul's letter being read. He glanced around the assembly that was crammed into his spacious home and he felt a real sense of satisfaction. Everything was going well; everything was in order.

"Good Order" was important to Philemon: he kept a close eye on his household accounts, going over them carefully each week with his household steward, checking all the debits and credits to make sure everything was in order. He looked across at his son, Septimus, now in his twenties, but still living at home. (Well property prices were so high and jobs so hard to find, it was far better having the lad at home, helping out with the family business, rather than struggling to survive like so many of his friends.) It wasn't always easy, mind you; Philemon sometimes became a bit impatient with his son, and for his part, Septimus had been known to complain to his mother about "Dad always being on my case! Sometimes, it seems that I can't do anything to please him."

Philemon looked next at his wife Apphia sitting beside him. She really was a good wife—exemplary, even. It was she who had suggested that they should open their home to make it the regular meeting place for the Christ-followers in Colossae and week by week she welcomed the guests with real warmth. She understood Philemon and made sure that her part of the household management was in line with his wishes.

No, everything was in order, like a well-presented set of accounts, all payments duly received. The letter from Paul, Philemon thought, was really the bonus entry that made the balance even healthier. Paul had even persuaded Philemon's runaway slave, Onesimus, to return. Philemon made a mental note that he would deal with Onesimus later: there was still some reckoning to be done about certain items that disappeared from the house at the time of Onesimus's departure. That could wait.

Onesimus was standing with the household slaves and field slaves at the back of the gathering. Philemon had heard recently that more than a third of the people in the Lycus Valley were slaves and that most of them had been born in households where their mothers were slaves.

Philemon thought for a moment about the words that Merring-Petros had read, "There is no distinction between Gentiles and Jews . . . barbarians, savages, slaves and free citizens—but Christ is all; Christ is in all." (Col 3:11). And again, "You are all the people of God; chosen and loved by as God's own." (Col 3:12). Philemon realized that he needed to think some more about what that all meant, but that would have to wait, because Merring-Petros was continuing:

"Wives, submit to your husbands, as fitting in the Lord—that is what you should do as Christians." (Col 3:18). Philemon relaxed even more; the Apostle is really wise, he thought, he knows the importance of good order. Then Philemon leaned forward as he heard the next words and interpreted them: "Husbands, love your wives—sacrifice your own interests for their welfare; exercise self-giving love for the good of your wife—and do not be harsh with them; do not harbour feelings of bitterness or resentment towards them." (Col 3: 19).

Philemon realized that the Apostle was giving a new twist to the Classical Household Codes that Philemon had been accustomed to. This new Code had some different emphases.

## Mutuality.

Up till now, most of the rights had been granted to men in their roles as husbands, parents and masters: now there was a call for *Matrimonial Mutuality*.

This meant that the submission that was asked of wives would not mean subordination; it was more than balanced by the commitment of the husband to love in the same way that Christ loved the Church. It would not, therefore, be a question of one being superior and the other inferior; rather the relationship would be built on Shared Commitment—on each allowing the other to have and fulfil their respective responsibility; and on Shared Care, each exercising the same self-giving love for the good of the other.

In many parts of our world, there continues to be high levels of verbal and physical abuse of women and, sadly, it is clear that men in the Church are also perpetrators of that violence and abuse. Too many men seem to see it as part of the "natural order" for them to use their greater physical strength or their economic advantages to threaten and intimidate women. This is not the way of Christ: among the followers of Christ differences of gender do not lead to greater rights and privileges for one group at the expense of the other, "here there is neither male nor female, because you are all one in Christ."

The Apostle applied the principle of mutuality into the wider family relationships and advocated *Familial Mutuality*. Whilst children were expected to Accept Discipline, "Children, it is your Christian duty to obey your parents, for that is what pleases the Lord" (v 20), parents needed to Avoid Discouragement: "parents do not provoke, irritate, or fret your children—do not be hard on them or harass them; lest they become discouraged and sullen, and morose and feel inferior and frustrated; do not break their spirit."[1]

Philemon squirmed in his chair, but he kept on listening to hear what the Apostle would say about mutuality in the world of work. *Occupational Mutuality*.

*For Slaves—Diligence in Work*. Philemon applauded the Diligence that Paul urged slaves to show: "obey your human masters—not only when their eyes are on you, because you want to get their approval . . . Whatever you do, work at it with all your heart as if you were working for the Lord and not for men." (Col 3:22).

*For Masters—Dignity of Workers*. "Masters (on your part) deal with your slaves fairly, knowing that you also have a Master in heaven." (Col 4:1).

This was a new idea for Philemon; the law told him that he could do whatever he liked with his slaves—determine their work and living conditions; beat them; brand them; even have them executed. Now the Apostle was telling him that he had to treat them justly and fairly, just as he would expect to be treated by God.

---

1. Amplified New Testament

Philemon couldn't help feeling that the requirement of Mutuality was going to be quite challenging for him. But before he could marshal his counter arguments, he saw that the Apostle had built his case very carefully and that the mutuality he urged was a corollary of the second principle in the new code.

## Integrity

All that he was asking of the church in Colossae arose from the premise, "Since you have been raised with Christ." (Col 3:1). It was in line with the Apostle's desire expressed at the start of his letter, "That you will be able to live as the Lord wants and will always do what pleases him," that is, that you live in holiness.

The criterion of Integrity meant having *Attitudes that Reflect Aspirations*.

Compassion (towards all people); kindness; humility; gentleness; patience; forgiveness; and above all, Love. These were the attitudes that would show whether aspirations were still earth-bound, or whether they had a spiritual and eternal focus.

Integrity also meant having *Actions that Renew the Aspirations*.

Intentions had to be made real in actions: "submit . . . love . . . obey . . . encourage . . . work with all your heart . . . "

There was a need for consistency between what the Christians professed and what they practised; their lives needed to be whole, to have Integrity as well as Mutuality.

As Philemon kept listening, he saw a third dimension of the new Code.

## Accountability.

There were two phrases that kept recurring, "In the Lord" and "To the Lord."

*In the Lord.* Paul saw this as the defining environment for the Christian; wherever they lived, whatever their occupation, they were and remained "in Christ"; they had a shared spiritual life, with Christ and with one another, because they were all in Christ.

Being the Body of Christ, living as the current expression of the will and purpose of God, we need to ensure that our values and our actions are inspired by, and energised by, the passions of Christ; and that they flow from our experience of Christ being in us and our being in Christ.

*To the Lord.* "Whatever you do, do it as if you are doing it as service to Jesus, your Lord." (Col 3:23). Our accountability should not only be in accord with what we claim about our realm of living, "in Christ," it should also recognise that we are called to give a reckoning, to make our "stewardship returns" to the Lord. It means taking seriously and acting responsibly to address the demeaning and exploitation of women and children and vulnerable members of our community, so that we can give an account to Christ, the One in whose image they are made.

The longest section of our reading for today deals with the relationship of slaves and masters. Philemon owned slaves. Onesimus, who had run away as a slave, had returned to Philemon's household with a letter of commendation from the Apostle Paul himself, in which the Apostle urged Philemon to accept Onesimus, and to regard him no longer as a belonging, a piece of property, but as a brother in Christ. This was a huge demand.

In his commentary on the Letter to the Colossians in the Daily Bible Study series[2], William Barclay suggests that one reason this section deals with the master-slave relationship in such length, and in much greater detail than the other two areas, is that it was the relationship that in Paul's eyes most comprehensively represented the relationship of Christ and the Church.

As slaves derived their identity from their masters, so Christians know themselves through their relationship with Christ; as slaves recognise that their destiny is in the hands of their masters, so Christians are to entrust themselves to Christ, "the Lord, who will give you as a reward that which he has kept for his own people." (Col 3:24). And there is the paradox, for under Greek and Roman law, slaves could not be inheritors; that was a privilege afforded only to sons. Now Christians of all backgrounds are being told that they

---

2. William Barclay, *The Letters to the Philippians, Colossians, and Thessalonians*, Daily Study Bible (Edinburgh: St Andrew's, 1970), 193.

are "joint-heirs with Christ" and will share God's inheritance, partake of God's holiness, because it had been credited to them.

Ignatius was a Bishop of Antioch, who was martyred in about 107CE. As he was taken under guard from Antioch to Rome to face his execution, he wrote letters to various churches, including one to the church in Ephesus. In that letter, he referred to their "beloved Bishop, Onesimus", and he uses the same play on words that Paul used in his letter to Philemon fifty years earlier. Onesimus means "useful", and both Paul and Ignatius wrote about how 'useful' Onesimus was in the work of Christ.

It is reasonable to surmise that Onesimus, once a runaway slave, became a beloved Bishop in Christ's Church. In his life he had come to recognise that his debits were more than he could ever cover by himself, and that his only credit was that which he could claim in Christ.

Have we looked at the debits and credits in our holiness account recently?

## A PRAYER

*Lord, save me from the pride that makes me think that I can increase my holiness balance through my own effort or goodness. With access to the unlimited resources of your eternal love and grace, help me to fulfil my responsibilities with diligence and with joy, showing generous love in all my relationships at home, or at work, that the realm of your holiness may grow. Amen.*

## CHAPTER 6

# Holiness: Together on the Journey.

### READ: COLOSSIANS 4:2-18.

### EXPLORE:

i. *Paul asks the church in Colossae to pray for him (4:2–4): what would you ask your fellow believers to pray for on your behalf?*
ii. *Paul has much to say about the place of prayer in the life of the church and the ministry of prayer offered by his fellow-workers: how could the prayer life of your church fellowship be improved? What would enable you to become more "adventurous" is your own praying?*
iii. *Paul urges the members to "Be wise in the way you act towards those who are not believers and use every opportunity you have . . . " What might this mean for you in your life at home and in the neighbourhood, and for your church community?*
iv. *Make a list of all the different people Paul mentions in Col 4:7–17 and notice what he says about each one. What else do we know about these people? Which of them challenges you the most?*
v. *Archippus is to be encouraged "To finish the task . . . given in the Lord's service (Col 4:17)." With the help of friends, identify or clarify, the task that you have been given in the Lord's service.*

vi. *Paul concludes the letter with his personal signature and a personal greeting: if you were writing to fellow members at your church, how would you describe yourself as you sign the letter and what would your greeting be?*

## DRAWING TOGETHER

If there is one thing that you can be sure about as a follower of Christ, it is that you will not make it on your own—and the good news is that you do not have to. The Call to Holiness is a call to being connected.

As Desmond Tutu has often said, "The self-sufficient human is an incomplete human.[1]" We are created for community; made by love and for love; and that applies most particularly to those who are part of the Church, the community of Christ's followers. We all need a little help from our friends.

In this final section of the Apostle's letter, we discover three kinds of help that we can offer to one another—and that we should be able to expect from one another as we journey into the holiness of being in communion with God and in community with others.

## Praying

This is such a valuable and yet so sadly under-rated ministry. It is a precious thing to be able to bring someone into the presence of God and to just hold them there lovingly and positively. Paul points to some of the marks of the Praying that we offer:

*Active (perhaps even Addictive).* "Be persistent in prayer." "Keep on praying; don't stop praying." (Col 4:2). And when prayer doesn't seem to be "working", that is the time to pray even more!

*Attentive.* "Keep alert as you pray." (Col 4:2b). Be like a watchman on duty, aware of what is happening, even as you pray. The three disciples who were closest to Jesus found it so hard to follow this discipline of prayer. On the Mount of Transfiguration and in

---

1. Heard in address given in "Birmingham Live," Birmingham UK, 1989.

the Garden of Gethsemane, two of the most critical times of Jesus' life, they are found asleep, when they should have been alert and watchful.

*Appreciative.* "Giving thanks to God." (Col 4:2c). It is possible for us to be so concerned about what we want to ask God for, that we do not show due thankfulness for all that we have been given already. Adoration—acknowledging who God is; praise—being awed by what God is like; thanksgiving—showing appreciation for what God has done; all of this enriches and enhances our relationship with God and makes our praying with one another and for one another so much more meaningful.

*Adventurous.* "Pray for us that God will give us a good opportunity to preach the message about the mystery of Christ." (Col 4:3).

Paul is in prison. It would be natural and expected for him to ask his friends to pray that he might be given a fair trial and that he might be released, but that is not Paul's request: he asks them to pray that there will be an opening for him to proclaim the message of Christ.

How adventurous are we in our prayers? Do we dare to imagine and ask for the things that would advance the spread of the Gospel and make its impact more telling, even when those requests seem almost ludicrous? Do we dare to take the rough mountain paths of prayer, rather than merely strolling by the quiet streams?

Christ encouraged his disciples to be both bold and persevering in their prayers. We help one another by praying for, and praying with, one another: making our prayers active, attentive, appreciative, and adventurous.

As we offer our prayers, we should be ready for the answers that will be given and that means prayer should be followed by putting into practice that which we pray for.

## Practising

If we pray for an opportunity to spread the good news, we have to make sure that we are ready to make the most of the opportunity when it arises; if we pray for boldness, we should not be taken aback when we find ourselves in a situation where courage is called for. As we pray for one another, we can also help one another prepare for and put into practice the answer to prayer.

The Apostle offers some guidelines for the way we engage after prayer:

*Discretion.* "Be wise in the way you act towards those who are not believers," (Col 4:5). It is good for believers to be "missionary minded", but it is important for us to be wise in knowing when to use words and when to let our attitudes and actions speak. It is discretion that enables the Gospel to be seen as offer, rather than threat. It is not enough just to have the right answer, says the Apostle, "you should know the right way of answering as well." (Col 4:6b).

And with Discretion, there needs to be *Discernment.* "Make good use of every opportunity that you have." (Col 4:5b).

Being alert as we pray means that we are more likely to recognise the opportunities to offer Christ which will come our way. Jesus spoke of the importance of "reading the signs of the age" and of recognising the quality of the soil that we are farming. As we go about our daily business, how conscious are we of the signs of spiritual hunger that people might display, sometimes quite unconsciously? How aware are we of the searching and longings that are expressed in the course of ordinary, everyday conversations? We can help one another with discernment.

But perhaps the characteristic that takes us by surprise (though it should not, as it has been a recurrent feature of the Letter) is *Delight.*

"Your speech should always be pleasant and interesting" (Col 4: 6). Now there's a challenge for everyone who wants to tell the Good News! How have we managed to make the most mind-blowing story ever told seem about as exciting as reading from a telephone directory? There is so much we all need to learn about the ways of communicating the message we have received—"Christ in you, the hope of glory"—and to communicate it in ways that make sense and bring delight. As we talk with one another about what we have discovered in Christ, we find that we begin to overflow with the sheer joy of being put right with God.

## Partnering

The Apostle ends his letter with an account of the people who are providing him with encouragement and support in his ministry, many of them known to the assembly in Colossae. In doing so, he shows a number of ways in which we can also help one another:

*Sharing News.* "Tychicus, who is a faithful worker and fellow servant in the Lord's work, will give you all the news about me." (Col 4:7). Not everything can be said in a letter, sometimes it needs the filling in by word of mouth—provided that does not slide into gossip that helps neither the person spoken about, nor the person spoken to. The aim of Tychicus's words, says the Apostle, will be "to cheer you up," to increase the delight of the hearers.

And with Tychicus there is "Onesimus, that dear and faithful brother, who belongs to your group. They will tell you everything that is happening here." We need to allow room for us to hear from one another what God is doing, and to learn where God is working. What a moment it must have been for the church in Colossae as they listened to Onesimus's personal testimony of how, as a slave, he had been "rescued, redeemed, and forgiven".

*Standing Alongside.* Being there in solidarity with one another when there are difficulties. Paul drew strength and comfort from companions in prison: "Aristarchus, who is in prison with me, sends you his greetings." (Col 4:10). And he was encouraged by the witness and presence of those who shared his background: "Mark . . . and Joshua, also called Justus, send greetings also. These three are the only Jewish converts who work with me for the Kingdom of God, and they have been a great help to me."

*Sustaining by Supplication.* "Greetings from Epaphras, another member of your group and a servant of Christ Jesus. He always prays fervently for you." Epaphras was committed to fervent, passionate, persevering prayer; "wrestling in prayer" on behalf of his fellow believers as he asked God to strengthen them so that they would be able to stand firm and become mature, through submitting themselves to God's will.

*Showing Steadfastness.* "Luke, our dear doctor and Demas send you their greetings" (Col 4: 14). Luke is named repeatedly as a companion of Paul in his travels, and here he is still, being there, staying with the Apostle to the end. There is a contrast with Demas, who is mentioned only once more in the New Testament outside the Colossians-Philemon correspondence, in 2 Timothy 4:10, where the report is, "Demas has left me, because he loved the present world more."

Archippus is to be encouraged to show similar steadfastness: "Say to Archippus, be sure to finish the task you were given in the Lord's service." What the task was, we do not know, but we know that we each have a particular role to fulfil in Christ's service and that we, too, are called on to see it to completion.

*Sharing Hospitality.* This was a vital ministry in the early Church and one which travelling missionaries depended on greatly. Nympha offered hospitality to the Christians in Laodicea (Col 4:15) just as Philemon and Apphia did in Colossae. It was a mark of the early Church that homes were opened for the benefit of local and travelling members of the Body of Christ.

How reassuring to know that our fellow Christians are there for us: ordinary people who do simply and faithfully the things that they are called to do in the service of the Master—praying, practising, partnering, that the Body of Christ might continue to be built up.

The Letter to the Church in Colossae begins with a greeting of 'Grace and Peace'. The Apostle goes on to commend the church for their 'faith, hope and love', the essential marks of Christ's followers. But he knows that as disciples there is still much for them to learn and more for them to become if they are to experience the depth and fullness of being in Christ and of living out the mystery, "Christ in you, the hope of glory".

It will be a challenge for every area of their lives—at home; at work; in their communities. It will require full-time commitment, stretching them mentally and spiritually and physically, as they seek to ensure that their whole lives reflect their commitment to Jesus, their Master, and can be offered with joy to him: "Whatever you do, in word or deed, do everything in the name of the Lord Jesus." (Col 3:17).

"Christ in you, the hope of glory" is the secret (an open secret) for fulfilled living, the secret of holiness. What a difference it would make—to our church, our families, our community, and to each of us personally—if, inspired by this Letter, we were able to discover the transforming power of that hope. Then, even if like the Apostle we might be 'in chains', as we signed off, the last words would echo the first, "Grace be with you. Amen."

## A PRAYER (BASED ON HYMN BY CHARLES WESLEY)

*O God of truth and love,*
*we choose your perfect way;*
*Ready your choice to approve,*
*your providence to obey;*
*Enter into your wise design—*
*and to your holiness incline.*

*Lord, you have made us one,*
*united all in you;*
*Your Word makes clear to us*
*the work that we should do:*
*So, may we in the world reveal*
*the holiness that is your will.*

www.ingramcontent.com/pod-product-compliance
Lightning Source LLC
Chambersburg PA
CBHW072035060426
42449CB00010BA/2280